A WALK ACROSS ENGLAND

A WALK OF 382 MILES IN 11 DAYS
FROM THE WEST COAST
TO THE EAST COAST OF ENGLAND

RICHARD LONG

With 130 illustrations in color

THAMES AND HUDSON

THE START AT THE EDGE

OF THE ATLANTIC OCEAN

SLOWER AND SMALLER

FOLLOWING A COW

CROSSING THE FIRST RIVER

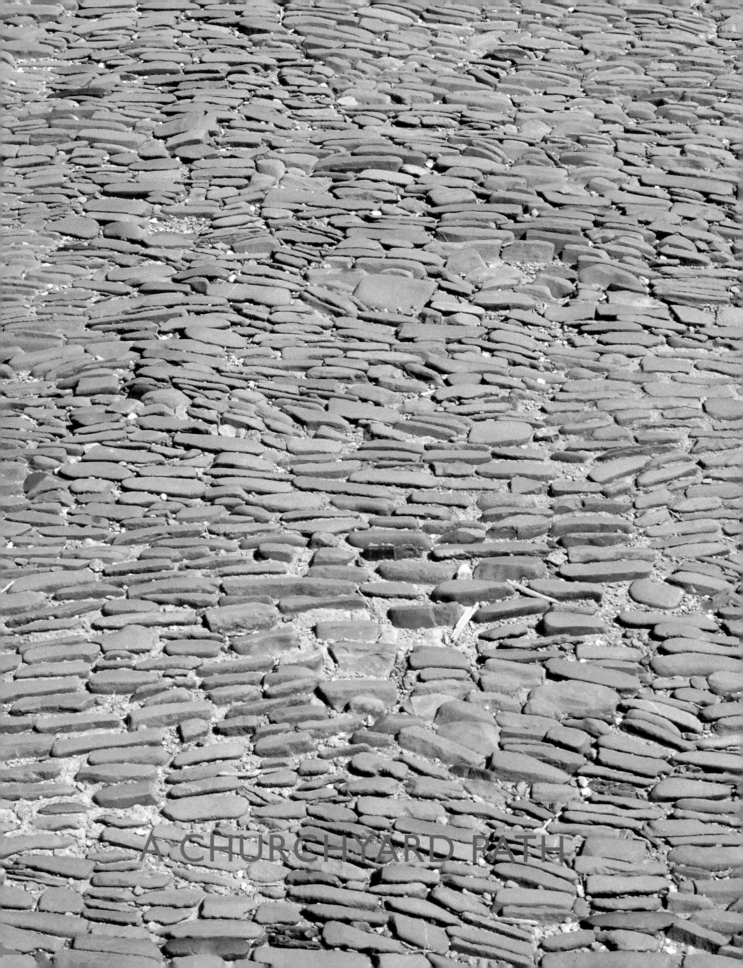

A CHURCHYARD PATH

DOWN

THE SECOND MIDDAY

AS CONCORDE FLIES OVERHEAD

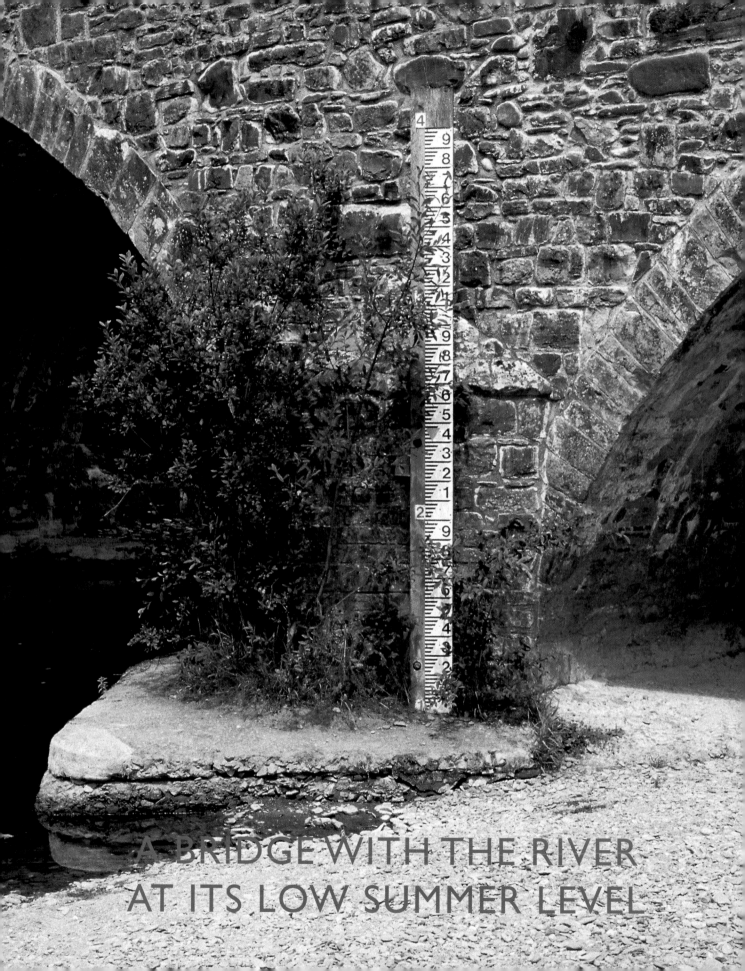

A BRIDGE WITH THE RIVER
AT ITS LOW SUMMER LEVEL

RESTING AND GAZING AND
SEEING A KETTLE IN THE CLOUDS

FOLLOWING THE HARVEST

A GOOD CROP OF MAIZE

AN ANIMAL HOLE AT THE ROADSIDE

HOT SUN

CLOUDS ON A WEST WIND

AND A RED FIELD

A BIRD DROPPING

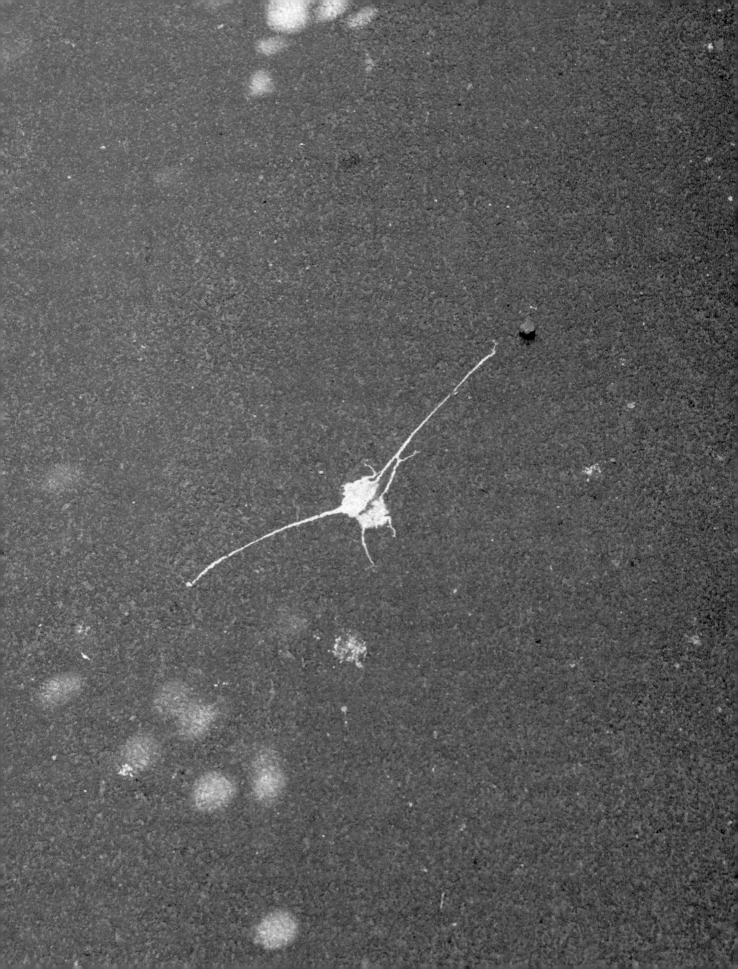

CROSSING A TIDAL RIVER

GOING THE RIGHT WAY

UP A LANE

TO THE TOP

AN EVENING DRINK

ANOTHER BIRD DROPPING
PROBABLY A SWAN

MY EVENING SHADOW

FEELING HUNGRY

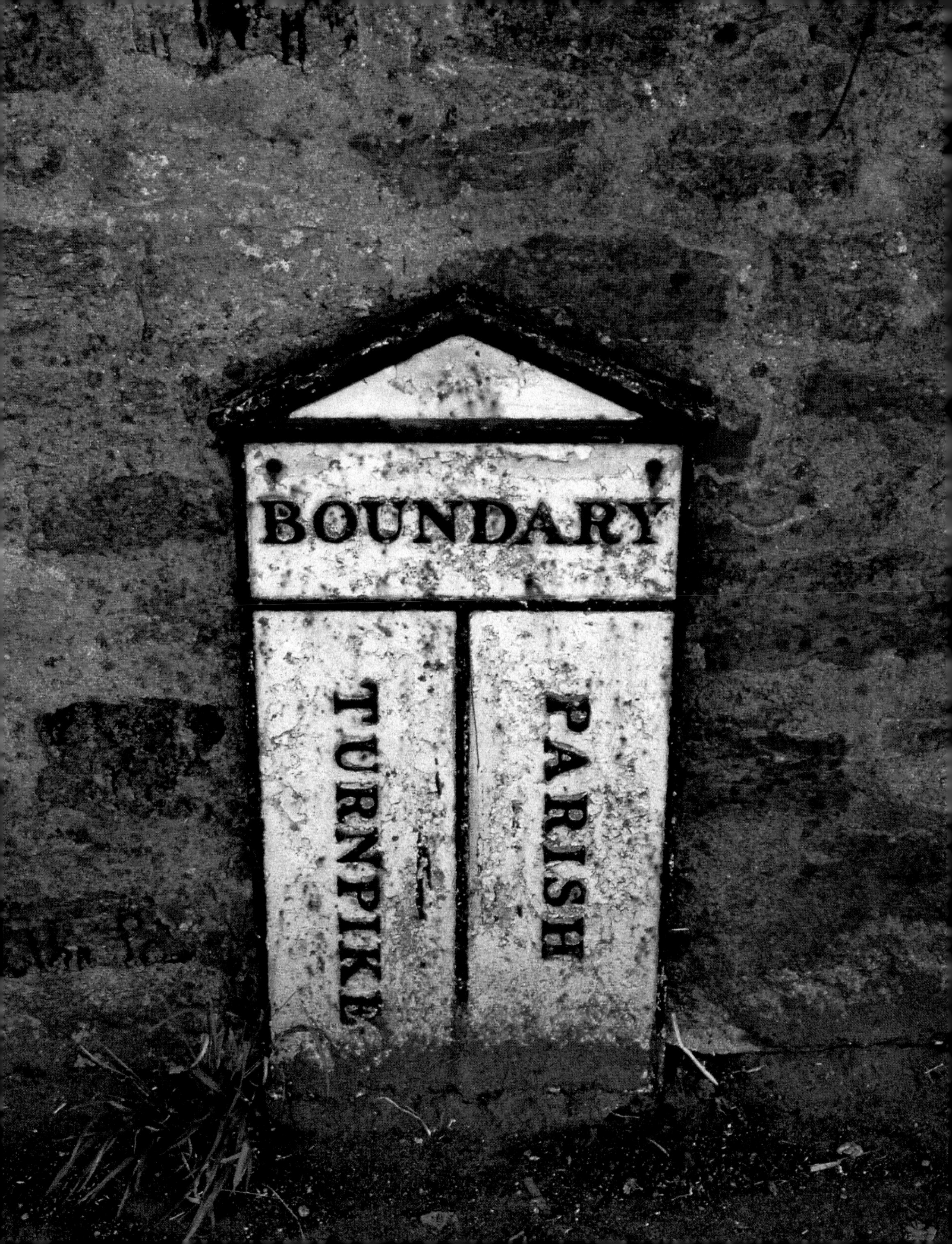
BOUNDARY
TURNPIKE
PARISH

A HORSE DRAWN ON A CHALK HILL

SACKS OF COAL BEING DELIVERED

WILD FLOWERS BY A WHEAT FIELD

CROSSING A RAIL LINE

AND A CANAL

ANOTHER CHALK HORSE

A STICKY LINE
THE ROAD MELTING IN THE HEAT

A COOL STREAM

STUNG BY NETTLES
WHILE PUTTING UP
AND TAKING DOWN MY TENT

PEE TRICKLING ACROSS THE ROAD

SPLASHING ALONG

IT'S STOPPED RAINING

A HORSE CHESTNUT LEAF

A FOOTPATH STILE

WET
PAINT

HERON

PASSING A CANAL LOCK

LISTENING TO THE SCREECH
OF YOUNG BUZZARDS
IN THE MORNING

THE SMELL OF FRESH SUMMER RAIN

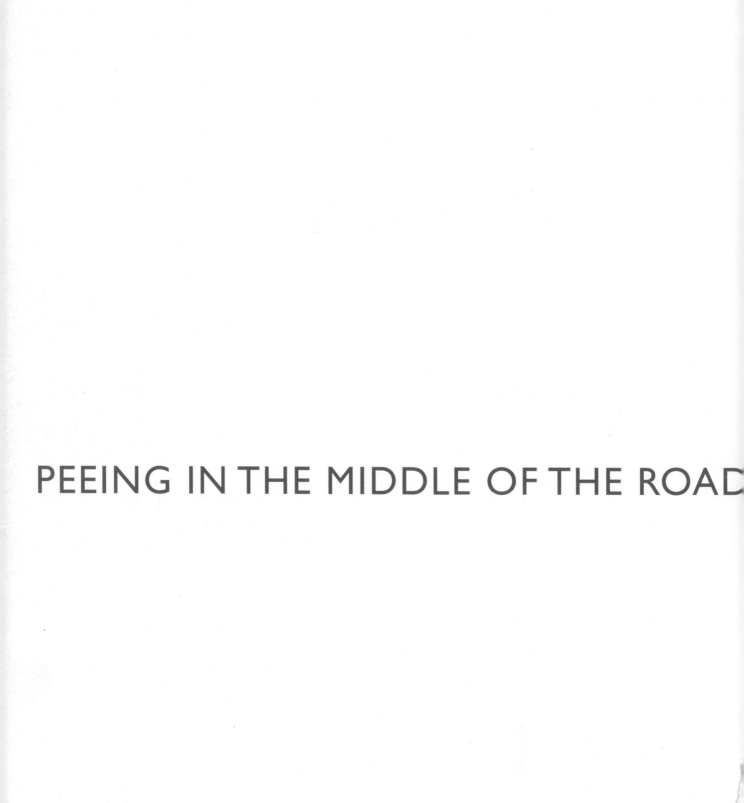

PEEING IN THE MIDDLE OF THE ROAD

THE SOUND OF COWS MUNCHING

THE RAIN SHADOW OF A TREE

RAIN CLOUDS

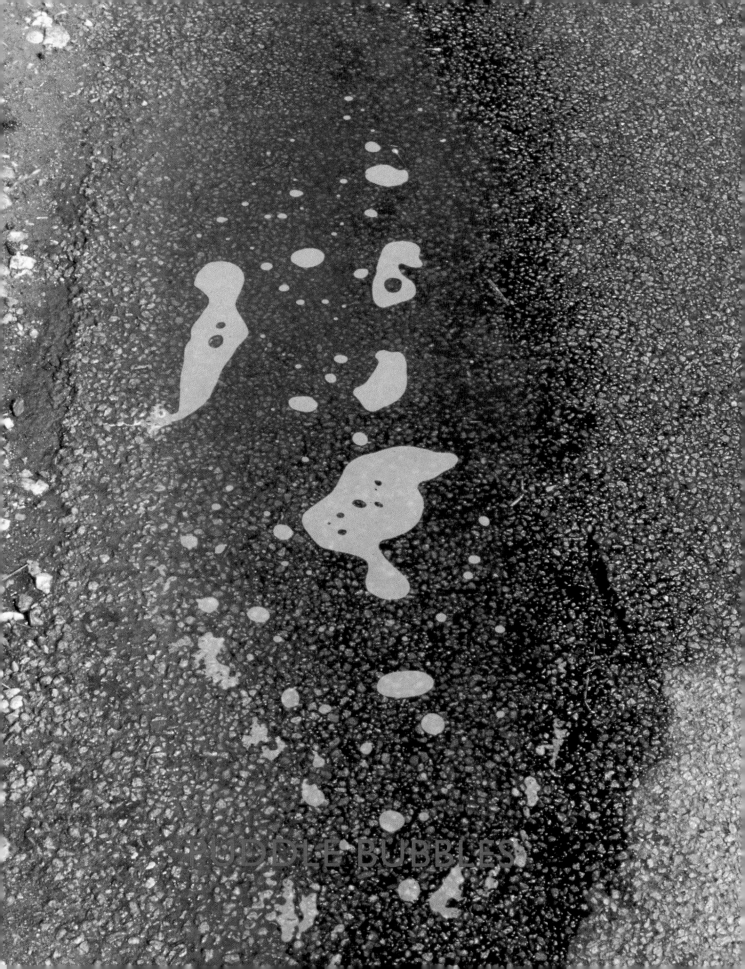

THE DISTANT SOUND
OF ROLLING THUNDER

THROWING A STONE INTO A POND

A SLOW-MOVING RIVER

WIND FLOWERS
SHE LOVES ME, SHE LOVES ME NOT

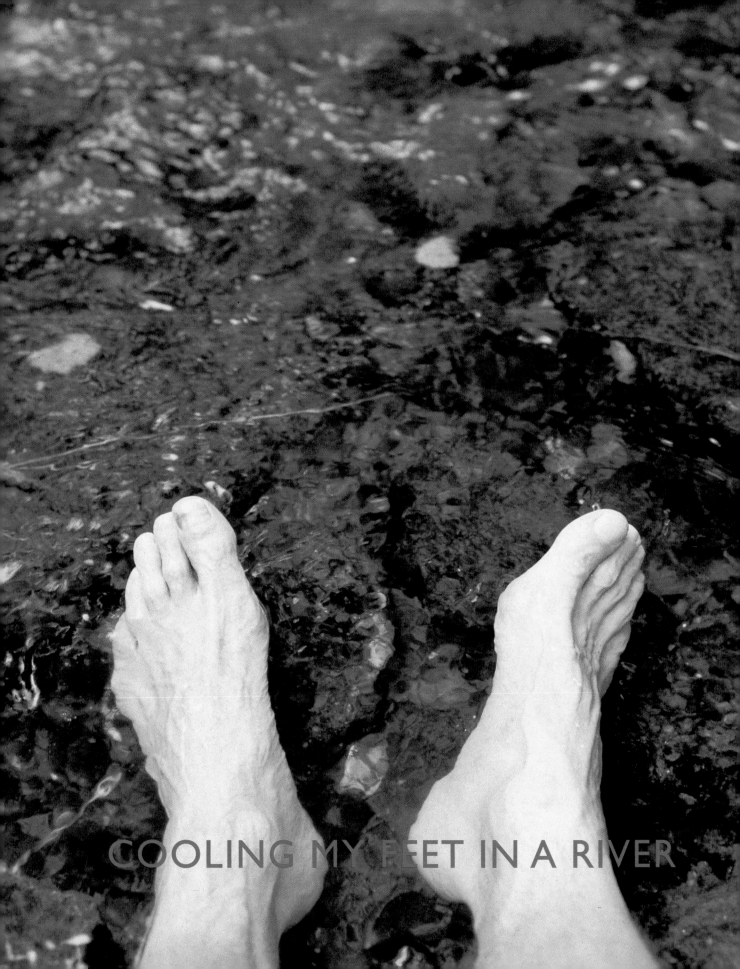

COOLING MY FEET IN A RIVER

FEELING THE HOT ROAD
ON MY BARE FEET

SMELLY SOCKS

A WINDMILL

A HOLLOW TREE

A FAMILY OF HORSES

THE FIRST PLOUGHED FIELD

WHISTLING ALONG

THE THREE PIGS

PINKS

OLD MAN'S BEARD

GETTING NEAR

MY LAST REST

THE END OF THE WALK
AT THE EDGE OF THE NORTH SEA

© 1997 Richard Long and 🐘 Children's Library Press, P. O. Box 2609,
Venice, California 90294, USA

First published in the United States of America in 1997 by
Thames and Hudson Inc., 500 Fifth Avenue, New York, New York 10110

Library of Congress Catalog Card Number 97-60275
ISBN 0-500-27976-4

Printed and bound in Hong Kong

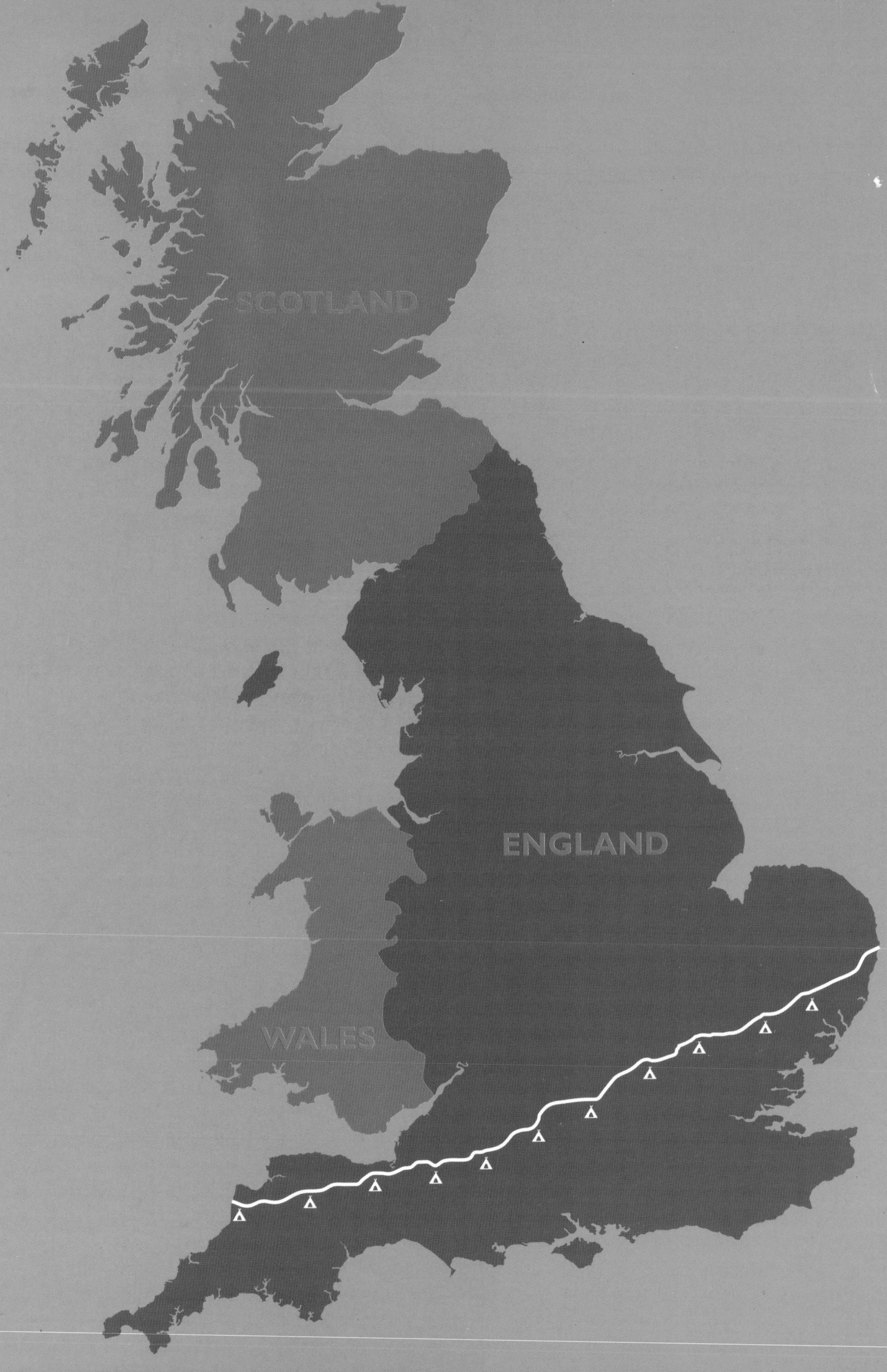

SCOTLAND
ENGLAND
WALES